Catechism

Catechism

Poems with cats by

Gail White

Kelsay Books

Cover: Illustration by Kate Greenaway
Dame Wiggins of Lee, and her seven wonderful cats
(public domain)

ISBN 13- 978-0692696668

Kelsay Books
White Violet Press
www.kelsaybooks.com

Acknowledgments

Poems in this collection have appeared in the following: *The Rotary Dial, The Lyric, Light Poetry Journal, Quest, New Verse News,* and *The Raintown Review.*

Contents

About the Author

Vain Question

What were you doing, my cats,
the day the burglars broke in?
They spared you, taking instead
the new TV and my rings.

We found the front door open
and you walking in and out.
I suspect you both looked on big-eyed,
never raised one shout

for help or called 911.
It must have seemed to you
just another of those strange things
that two-legged beings do.

So the burglars did their job
and departed, unfoiled, uncursed.
We called the police next day,
but we fed you first.

Cats Abroad

*It is not worth the while to go round the world
to count the cats in Zanzibar.*
—Thoreau

The cats of England at the cottage door
look up expectant, when the milk man comes,
like furry Olivers who ask for more,
beneath a shelter of chrysanthemums.

The cats of Belgium in the baker's shop
adorn a window—in the bar, a stool.
The cats of Greece, at every culture stop,
are looking for a tourist to befool.

I judge the nations by the way they treat
these purry gentry just below their knees.
Where cats are loved, I know that strangers meet
a kindly welcome and a will to please.

Why spend so much and haul myself so far
if not to count the cats in Zanzibar?

Reality Show

The cat says, Pay me some attention,
you dumb people, even though
you have more troubles than you can mention

clamoring for your intervention.
Where did your education go?
Even the cat would have paid attention

to your last credit card suspension,
your negative cash and credit flow.
The aggravations you could mention

include your child's incomprehension
of every song and dance you know.
The cat has paid you more attention

than this dumb kid whose reprehension
of your whole life will only grow.
The other troubles you could mention

include the loss of your old age pension,
your job, your sex life, last year's snow.
And through each trial that you can mention,
the cat's demanding your attention.

Fat Cat

My cat, no Lassie, looks at me
with eyes whose green tranquility
could watch me drown as long as she
had just been fed. She ought to be
a grand Episcopalian cat
with bluejay feathers on her hat,
who flips her furs across the pew,
complacently ignoring you.
A cat who gets her every wish,
who knows what wine to have with fish,
imposingly, serenely fat,
a white-gloved Southern Lady cat.

For cats who have a sense of worth,
there is no higher form of birth.
We rather may anticipate
to reach the nobler feline state
where fame and wealth are trivial things,
to purr on Popes and shed on kings.

Do Cats Have Souls?

My human friend, consult your heart.
I think you surely cannot mean
that like that raving bore Descartes
you think I'm just a soft machine?

Pleasure is human—don't I purr?
Playing is human—I can play.
To err is human—I can err.
You don't need goldfish, anyway.

If there's a human Paradise,
be sure I'll follow at your heels
(unless distracted by the mice
that romp in the Elysian Fields).

The Solitary Woman

In a tiny cottage called the Laurel Tree
the woman lived alone. Nobody came
to see her and she had no family,
so week by week her life was much the same.
She went to church and said the rosary,
took in the mail for neighbors out of town,
adopted cats, caught news on BBC,
and at a roll-top desk she wrote things down—
things no one ever saw, although we guessed
a novel, memoirs, poetry, and more—
but we saw nothing, though we did our best.
And when she died alone, at eighty-four,
with no companion but a big gray cat,
we pitied her. We were such fools as that.

Snake in the Bedroom

My cat brings in a smallish serpent,
nine inches long and pencil-thin,
knowing that I won't dare to touch it—
who knows where that snake's been?

The snake may starve behind the bookcase,
leaving its diamond-spotted skin
to be discovered in the dust
when braver souls move in.

I live surrounded by the dying.
I can't feel guilty all the time.
Snakes done to death by circumstances:
my sloth, another's crime.

The Devoted Creatures

Past the flaming sword of justice,
  like a scroll unfurled,
Dog and Cat, with Eve and Adam,
  ventured on the world.

"Have you followed me from Eden,
  You, my gentle cat?"
"No, I saw a mouse escaping,
  I ran after that."

"Have you followed me from Eden,
  faithful dog of mine?"
"Only because you could never
  keep that cat in line."

"Have you followed me from Eden,
  woman that God gave?"
"Someone has to feed the creatures -
  You can build a cave."

Cats, Dogs, and Plato

Cat is a mistress in a new mink stole.
Dog, a clown who begs for a drink.
Desire and pursuit of the whole
is love, says Plato. Dog might think
that you alone can complete his soul,
but Cat will calculate the link
between desire and self-control.
Cat writes her love with invisible ink.

Dog love is meek, cat love is tough.
Cat thinks you'll do, but she might look higher.
Dog never thinks he's loved enough,
his heart is a nodule of desire.
But Cat is whole in herself, and that
is why we grovel for love from a cat.

Traveling with Cats on a Snowy Evening

I've no idea whose woods these are,
but I'm not getting very far
from Albany to NYC
with two cats yowling in my car.

These blasted cats must think it queer
to stop without a sandbox near,
but listen, guys, I'm twice your size,
so use the woods or else, you hear?

They give their big round eyes a blink
to ask each other what they think,
and I can tell they'll make life hell,
and plan on driving me to drink.

The woods are looming dark and deep.
The car is slowing to a creep.
Why did I try to cross NY?
I'm breathing cat hairs while I sleep.

Lavinia Dickinson's Cat

In gray and silver vestments
   our presbyter presides,
a grave and silent hierarch
   who served the Ptolemies.

He makes of immobility
   a fortifying charm,
inscribing on the hearthrug
   his own cuneiform.

But any foe that wakens
   the Moloch in his heart
would better meet at Austerlitz
   a second Bonaparte.

The Devil's Deal

I met the devil out on a stroll
and gave him an offer for my soul.

"Money," I said, "is not my aim,
but give my writing immortal fame."

The devil gave me a small black cat
saying "Watch how it moves, and write like that."

I watched it run and I watched it play
and wrote more gracefully every day.

I poured out word after sparkling word
and the cat curled up in my lap and purred.

The devil came in the full moon's shine
with an author's contract for me to sign.

I said, "Go back the way you came.
I've changed my mind about deathless fame.

"Ambition comes from a heart gone dry.
Love keeps us busy, my cat and I."

Brother Dog, Sister Cat

by Gail White and Barbara Loots

Dog is dumber than a TV husband,
trusting as a cuckold in a Shakespeare play,
faithful as a nineteenth century butler,
sentimental as a drunk on New Year's Day.

Cat is cagy as a fortune teller,
loopy as a starlet in a nineteen-thirties role,
sensuous as smoke around a stripper,
elusive as conviction in the soul.

Abelard, or Love Gone Wrong

My altered cat runs out the door
and rackets round the yard.
Because he'll be a stud no more,
I call him Abelard.

But when he meets a lady cat
with soft and yielding paws,
he doesn't quite remember that
he's not the man he was.

He climbs her back and bites her neck—
he recollects the game.
But still he meets a fatal check:
results are not the same.

(How often, when romances end,
it puzzles cats and men
to know why last night's lady friend
will not step out again.)

Now other cats, with raucous glee,
cry out their mating song,
while Abelard sits home with me
and wonders what went wrong.

Walt Whitman Encounters the Cosmos with the Cats of New York

The cats of morning awaken, sultry and feral,
Ready to hunt, to mate, to kick some serious cat butt.
Their green and yellow eyes burst open as a child slits the top off a
pumpkin,

The alley cat is awake; the garbage can, last night's refuge, is
rudely up-ended.
The Vanderbilts' cat awakens on Vanderbilt's pillow.
It washes its face with a loud slurping noise.
The Vanderbilts do nothing; they are terrified of the thing.
The farm cat is up and about, looking for breakfast.
It falls on the field mice like Basil the Bulgar Slayer.
The actress's cat makes a nest in last night's costume.
It may as well go back to sleep. She won't be up
Until God knows when. The banker's cat is curled
In a neat little package, it purrs that interest is rising.
The mother cat moves her kittens from the back of the closet
To the fireplace, thinks better of it, moves half of them back,
Then sits in the hallway and says to hell with this motherhood
business.

Bastet is walking the streets and I walk with her.
I, Walt Whitman, companion of cats, have become all cats.
I look behind the restaurants for scraps of fish.
I rub myself on the legs of total strangers.
They run off screaming. They are not aware of my secret.
My brothers and sisters and I are watching the East'
The sun only rose this morning
Because my people are watching.

Alleygory

on the Feral Cat Neutering Program

He dwelt among the alleyways,
  He dined on mouse and dove.
A cat whom there were none to raise,
  To pamper, or to love.

A crabgrass, by a garbage can
  Half hidden from the eye,
Cursed as a Derby also-ran,
  Wild as a tsetse fly.

He lived unknown, and few could know
  What changed his mating whim,
But Lucifer is "fixed" —and O
  The difference to him!

She Compares Her Lover to Her Cat

While you're away, my love, I stroke instead
of you the dainty panther in my bed,
more exquisite than satin and more sleek
than rain, but sadly unequipped to speak.
You are my information source, my song,
my lover's lexicon—and yet how wrong
about your health, how vexed with what I write,
how testy at an unintended slight!
The panther only purrs—but you, my mate,
how can you be so damned articulate
yet lack the sense to come in when it rains?
If only you had fur and she had brains.

Karma

after Thomas Hardy, "During Wind and Rain"

When I was filthy rich,
Hey ho, offshore accounts!
Little I thought that I
Would be taxed for obscene amounts
And that stocks would nosedive and die.
Ah no, the times go,
Money is naught but a fickle bitch.

I married a trophy wife,
Hey ho, fabulous sex!
Little I thought that she
Would write such voluminous checks
I'd be driven to bankruptcy—
Ah no, the times go,
How soon I tired of married life!

I bought me a Persian cat,
Fat, sleek, beautiful—purr!
Never a cat in town
Was in beauty equal to her
Or so quick to garner renown.
Ah no, the times go,
My lungs are pockets of snow-white fur.

Cat Hoarder

My children think I have too many cats.
I don't agree, but I know what it means.
They think I'm getting senile, breeding bats
in this old belfry. Children don't know beans.
Wait till they're old and see their crepey skin
like washed unironed taffeta, their veins
a railway map of Europe, while they spin
unheard-of nightmares in diminished brains.
Before your body is a nuisance more
than a delight, before you'd welcome death
sooner than one more catheter, before
June weather chills you with December's breath
and your unlovely skin needs warmer furs,
my dears, you'll love what sits on you and purrs.

Saint Francis Preaches to the Cats, Who Pay No Attention

You cats and kittens, praise the Lord
who gave you claws to be your sword,
who clothed you with his softest fur
and graced you with your gracious purr.

He made you hunters without peer,
attentive both in eye and ear.
But when you take your prey alive,
be merciful—spare one in five.

They listened, but with hearts reserved.
They thought his praises well deserved.
But when he turned to good advice,
their eyelids fell. They dreamed of mice.

Balladette of Stray Cats

Why do the stray cats always head for me?
I've tried discouragement, but still they come.
The sense that here the entertainment's free,
My will is weak, one mew and I'm their chum.
And I know where this latest lot is from—
Four little tuxies, rather short and fat.
Their dad's a stranger, but I know their mum.
WHEN are my neighbors going to spay their cat?

Neighbors, these episodes are worrisome.
Every few months a new male's up at bat.
I cry to all the gods that life is rum.
WHEN are my neighbors going to spay their cat?

The Candidate Withdraws

These are the days of famine,
the times that try men's souls.
I've spent a third of the money
and I'm nowhere in the polls.

I'm rejoining the middle classes
who think I'm out of touch.
I'm spending time with my family
though I never liked them much.

What I can't say on the record
—though I think it for all that—
is "Screw you, John Q. Public,
and your children and your cat."

Elegy in April

Spring's back again, riding a surge of death.
My cats, the heralds of the holocaust,
leave lizards underfoot, and birds whose breath
their claws have stopped lie wrapped in Spanish moss
outside the door. The moth and dragonfly
now writhe exhausted in the spider's web.
But there's an upside too. The bayou's high
and mallard ducks are mating, neb to neb.
On cultivated ground, the golden wound of
roses is an ever-new surprise,
and last year's caterpillars, long cocooned,
are winging toward the hedge as butterflies.
This resurrection, though, it not for men.
We're annuals. We don't come up again.

Departure

They have paid all they have
to enter this cramped space.
They no more know
when they will sleep again
or where, than the blind
mole knows if it will escape
the cat outside its hole.
Universe, be kind.

On Louisiana Politics

The politician, like the tabby's young,
Attempts to clean his backside with his tongue.

About the Author

Gail White is a formalist poet with work in many journals, including *Measure, Light, First Things,* and *Hudson Review.* She is a two-time winner of the Howard Nemerov Sonnet Award. Her latest book, Asperity Street, was published in 2015 by Able Muse Press. She lives in Breaux Bridge, Louisiana, with her husband Arthur and cats, Tuxy, Quercus, Rabbit, Gray Blimp, and Five Spot.

Made in the USA
Coppell, TX
27 September 2021